CORONARY ARTERY DISEASE

REVERSE

COOKBOOK

Quick and Easy Heart Healthy, Low Sodium Recipes to Reduce Cholesterol and Unclog Blocked Arteries

DR. KADEN WINTON

Would you like to get deeper insights about this book, or do you have questions that may arise from using this book: kindly send a mail to us @ wintonconsults@gmail.com

Table of Contents

Introduction

A man named James lived in a small town nestled amidst rolling hills. He was a loving husband, father, and hardworking individual who dedicated his life to providing for his family. James had always taken pride in his health and believed he led a balanced lifestyle. However, fate had different plans for him when he received the devastating news of being diagnosed with coronary artery disease.

The diagnosis shook James to the core. Thoughts of his family's future, the uncertainty of his well-being, and the fear of what lay ahead consumed him. Determined to fight for his health and regain control of his life, James relentlessly searched for answers. He scoured the internet, read medical journals, and consulted with various healthcare professionals.

Amidst his research, James stumbled upon a post that caught his attention—about healing coronary heart disease through the power of diet. Intrigued by the promise of a natural approach to healing, he delved deeper into the topic. The post led him to a book titled "The Coronary Artery Disease

Reverse Cookbook," written by a passionate author who shared her journey and the transformative power of food. Without hesitation, James purchased the book and eagerly delved into its pages. As he read through the chapters, he discovered a wealth of knowledge about the impact of nutrition on heart health. The book provides a comprehensive meal plan to reverse coronary artery disease, incorporating heart-healthy ingredients and delicious recipes.

Motivated by hope and with newfound knowledge, James began implementing the meal plan into his daily life. He replaced processed foods with whole, nutritious ingredients, indulged in colorful fruits and vegetables, and incorporated heart-healthy fats. Gradually, his kitchen transformed into a sanctuary of healing, where every meal was prepared with love and purpose.

Weeks turned into months, and James started noticing subtle changes within himself. He had more energy, his cholesterol levels stabilized, and his weight gradually decreased. But it wasn't just the physical changes that amazed him; it was the profound sense of well-being he experienced. His mind felt clearer, and his spirit felt lighter.

As time went on, James went for regular check-ups with his doctor. The results were astounding. His cardiac function had improved significantly, and his doctor admired James's progress. They marveled at how James had embraced the healing power of food and transformed his life through simple dietary changes.

James's journey was not just about reversing his coronary artery disease; it was about reclaiming his vitality, embracing a newfound appreciation for life, and inspiring others to do the same. He shared his story with friends, family, and even strangers, spreading awareness about the transformative power of nutrition.

Today, James continues to thrive, cherishing each day as a gift. His journey serves as a reminder that, with determination, knowledge, and the right tools, we can take control of our health and reverse the course of the disease. Through the pages of *"The Coronary Artery Disease Reverse Cookbook"* and his unwavering determination,

James rewrote his health story, turning it into a tale of hope, resilience, and the incredible healing power of food.

Imagine living with the constant fear of a fragile heart, the pain that radiates through your chest, and the limitations it places on your life. Coronary artery disease, a silent and formidable enemy, affects millions of individuals worldwide, leaving them desperate for a solution that can restore their health and vitality.

Suppose you have been diagnosed with coronary artery disease. In that case, you understand the toll it takes on your physical and emotional well-being. The limitations it imposes on your daily life, the fear that lingers with every heartbeat, and the endless cycle of medications and treatments can leave you feeling helpless and trapped.

But what if there was a way to break free from the clutches of this disease? What if you could take control of your health and reverse the damage to your heart? The answer lies within the transformative power of nutrition and the revolutionary approach presented in "The Coronary Artery Disease Reverse Cookbook."

This book is not just another diet plan but a beacon of hope, offering a comprehensive solution to combat coronary artery disease and reclaim your life. By harnessing the healing potential of specific foods and adopting a strategic dietary approach, you can rewrite the course of your health and experience a profound transformation.

Within these pages, you will discover a carefully curated collection of recipes, meal plans, and invaluable insights that will empower you to make informed dietary choices. This book is your guide, showing you how to nourish your body with the right ingredients, unlock the healing power of nutrition, and revolutionize your approach to food.

Gone are the days of restrictive diets and bland meals. The recipes in *"The Coronary Artery Disease Reverse Cookbook"* are delicious and designed to support your heart health. From hearty breakfasts to vibrant lunches and satisfying dinners, every dish is crafted with a deep understanding of the nutrients your body needs to thrive.

This book, however, is more than just a collection of recipes. It is a road map to reclaiming your health, giving you the knowledge, tools, and strategies to make long-term changes. You will learn about the role of nutrition in reversing coronary artery disease, uncover the powerful benefits of specific nutrients, and gain practical tips for incorporating heart-healthy choices into your daily life.

Remember that you are not alone as you embark on this transformative journey. We will navigate the challenges, celebrate our victories, and support one another. With dedication, determination, and guidance in this book, you can pave a new path to healing, vitality, and a life free from the limitations of coronary artery disease.

Are you ready to embark on this life-changing journey? Prepare to embrace the power of nutrition, reclaim your heart health, and rediscover the joy of living a vibrant and fulfilling life. It is time to break free from the grip of coronary artery disease and take control of your destiny. Let the pages of *"The Coronary Artery Disease Reverse Cookbook"* be your roadmap to a healthier heart and a brighter future.

The 21-Day Meal Plan for Coronary Health

Welcome to the 21-Day Meal Plan for Coronary Health! This comprehensive meal plan supports your journey toward reversing coronary artery disease and promoting a healthy heart. By following this meal plan, you will discover various delicious recipes specifically crafted to nourish your body, provide essential nutrients, and support your overall well-being.

What sets the recipes in this meal plan apart is their focus on heart-healthy ingredients and the inclusion of key nutrients essential for healing and maintaining a strong cardiovascular system. Each recipe has been carefully designed to provide optimal nutrition while considering taste and enjoyment.

One of the key factors in managing and reversing coronary artery disease is adopting a wholesome and balanced diet that focuses on nourishing the body with nutrient-rich foods. The recipes in this meal plan are thoughtfully crafted to incorporate ingredients known to have cardiovascular benefits and promote heart health.

These recipes are abundant in key nutrients such as omega-3 fatty acids, fiber, antioxidants, and phytochemicals, all of which play vital roles in reducing inflammation, improving blood flow, maintaining healthy cholesterol levels, and supporting overall heart health. You will find various ingredients like fresh fruits, vegetables, whole grains, lean proteins, and healthy fats that synergize to nourish your body and promote cardiovascular wellness.

Throughout this 21-day journey, you will discover the pleasure of preparing and savoring wholesome meals that taste delightful and contribute to your well-being. By following the provided meal plan, you will experience a variety of flavors, textures, and culinary delights, ensuring that your healing journey is effective and enjoyable.

It's important to note that this meal plan is intended as a guide and can be tailored to suit your individual preferences and dietary needs. You are encouraged to listen to your body, make adjustments as necessary, and consult with a healthcare professional or nutritionist for personalized advice.

Get ready to embark on this transformative journey towards better coronary health. The 21-Day Meal Plan for Coronary Health is your roadmap to nourishing your body, embracing a heart-healthy lifestyle, and discovering the power of food as medicine. Let's begin this culinary adventure and empower ourselves to reverse coronary artery disease one delicious meal at a time!

As you dive into this transformative culinary experience, it's essential to arm yourself with a well-prepared grocery shopping list. This comprehensive list will ensure that you have all the necessary ingredients at your fingertips, making your cooking process seamless and enjoyable.

In this grocery shopping list, you'll find a carefully curated selection of heart-healthy ingredients that align with the recipes featured in the cookbook. Each item has been chosen for its nutritional value and its ability to support cardiovascular well-being. By stocking your pantry and refrigerator with these wholesome ingredients, you'll be well-prepared to create delicious and nourishing meals that promote optimal heart health.

Grocery Shopping List

1. **Fruits and Vegetables**:
- Apples
- Berries (strawberries, blueberries, raspberries)
- Citrus fruits (oranges, lemons)
- Leafy greens (spinach, kale, arugula)
- Cruciferous vegetables (broccoli, cauliflower, Brussels sprouts)
- Tomatoes
- Avocados
- Bell peppers
- Carrots

2. **Whole Grains and Legumes**:
- Whole wheat bread or wraps
- Brown rice
- Quinoa
- Oats
- Lentils
- Chickpeas
- Black beans

3. Lean Proteins:

- Skinless chicken breast
- Salmon or other fatty fish
- Tofu or tempeh
- Eggs

4. Healthy Fats and Oils:

- Extra virgin olive oil
- Avocado oil
- Nuts (almonds, walnuts, pistachios)
- Seeds (chia seeds, flaxseeds)

5. Dairy and Dairy Alternatives:

- Greek yogurt (low-fat or non-fat)
- Almond milk or other non-dairy milk

6. Herbs and Spices:

- Garlic
- Ginger
- Turmeric
- Cinnamon
- Basil
- Oregano

- Paprika
- Cumin

7. Other Essentials:

- Low-sodium vegetable or chicken broth
- Low-sodium soy sauce or tamari
- Balsamic vinegar
- Dijon mustard
- Honey or maple syrup (optional sweeteners)
- Dark chocolate (70% cocoa or higher)

Remember to check your pantry for any items you may already have before heading to the grocery store. Additionally, consider opting for organic and locally sourced ingredients whenever possible to further enhance the nutritional quality of your meals.

With this comprehensive grocery shopping list in hand, you're now equipped to embark on your heart-healthy culinary journey. Embrace the power of nutrition, savor the flavors of wholesome ingredients, and experience the joy of cooking meals that support your cardiovascular well-being.

Happy shopping and happy cooking!

Day 1:

Breakfast: Berry Oatmeal Bowl

Ingredients:

- ½ cup rolled oats
- 1 cup almond milk
- 1 tablespoon chia seeds
- ½ teaspoon vanilla extract
- ¼ cup mixed berries
- 1 tablespoon chopped nuts (almonds, walnuts, or pecans)

Preparation:

1. In a saucepan, combine rolled oats and almond milk. Cook over medium heat until the oats are soft, and the mixture thickens.

2. Stir in chia seeds and vanilla extract.

3. Transfer to a bowl and top with mixed berries and chopped nuts.

Lunch: Chickpea Salad Wrap

Ingredients:

- 1 cup rinsed and drained canned chickpeas
- ¼ cup diced cucumber
- ¼ cup diced bell pepper
- 2 tablespoons diced red onion
- 2 tablespoons chopped fresh parsley
- 2 tablespoons lemon juice
- 1 tablespoon extra-virgin olive oil
- Salt and pepper to taste
- Whole grain tortilla or wrap

Preparation:

1. In a bowl, mash the chickpeas with a fork or potato masher until slightly chunky.

2. Add cucumber, bell pepper, red onion, parsley, lemon juice, olive oil, salt, and pepper. Mix well.

3. Spread the chickpea salad onto a whole-grain tortilla or wrap. Roll it up and cut it in half if desired.

Dinner: Baked Salmon with Quinoa and Roasted Vegetables

Ingredients:

- 4 ounces salmon fillet
- ½ cup cooked quinoa
- Assorted roasted vegetables (such as broccoli, carrots, and cauliflower)
- Lemon wedges for garnish
- Fresh dill or parsley for garnish

Preparation:

1. Heat oven to 375 degrees Fahrenheit (190 degrees Celsius).

2. Place the salmon fillet on a parchment-lined baking sheet. Season to taste with salt, pepper, and lemon juice.

3. Bake for 15-20 minutes until the salmon is cooked.

4. Serve the baked salmon with cooked quinoa and roasted vegetables. Garnish with lemon wedges and fresh dill or parsley.

Snack: Greek Yogurt with Berries

Ingredients:

- ½ cup Greek yogurt
- Handful of mixed berries (strawberries, blueberries, raspberries)

Preparation:

1. In a bowl, spoon Greek yogurt.

2. Top with mixed berries.

3. Serve and enjoy

Day 2:

Breakfast: Veggie Scramble

Ingredients:
- ½ cup tofu, crumbled
- ½ cup mixed vegetables (such as bell peppers, spinach, and mushrooms)
- 2 tablespoons nutritional yeast
- ½ teaspoon turmeric
- Salt and pepper to taste
- 1 teaspoon olive oil

Preparation:
1. Warm the olive oil in a skillet over medium heat.
2. Add mixed vegetables and sauté until tender.
3. Add crumbled tofu, nutritional yeast, turmeric, salt, and pepper. Cook for another 3-5 minutes, stirring occasionally.
4. Serve the veggie scramble with whole grain toast or a side of fresh fruit.

Lunch: Quinoa Salad with Avocado Dressing

Ingredients:
- ½ cup cooked quinoa
- ½ cup mixed greens

- ¼ cup cherry tomatoes, halved

- ¼ cup diced cucumber

- 2 tablespoons diced red onion

- 1 tablespoon chopped fresh herbs (parsley, cilantro, etc.)

- For the avocado dressing:

- ½ ripe avocado

- Juice of 1 lime

- 1 tablespoon extra-virgin olive oil

- Salt and pepper to taste

- Water (if needed for desired consistency)

Preparation:

1. Combine cooked quinoa, mixed greens, cherry tomatoes, cucumber, red onion, and fresh herbs in a bowl.

2. Mash the avocado and lime juice together in a separate bowl until smooth.

3. Stir in olive oil, salt, and pepper. If required, add more water to achieve the desired consistency.

4. Drizzle the avocado dressing over the quinoa salad and toss to coat.

Dinner: Lentil Curry with Brown Rice

Ingredients:

- ½ cup cooked brown rice
- ½ cup cooked lentils
- ½ cup diced tomatoes
- ¼ cup diced onion
- 2 cloves garlic, minced
- 1 teaspoon curry powder
- ½ teaspoon turmeric
- ½ teaspoon cumin
- ¼ teaspoon cinnamon
- ½ cup coconut milk
- 1 tablespoon olive oil
- Fresh cilantro for garnish

Preparation:

1. Heat olive oil in a pan over medium heat.

2. Add diced onion and minced garlic. Sauté until fragrant and golden.

3. Stir in diced tomatoes, curry powder, turmeric, cumin, and cinnamon. Cook for 2-3 minutes.

4. Cooked lentils and coconut milk are added. Allow the flavors to blend for 10 minutes.

5. Serve the lentil curry over brown rice and garnish with fresh cilantro.

Snack: Carrot Sticks with Hummus

Ingredients:
- Carrot sticks
- 2 tablespoons hummus

Preparation:
1. Slice carrots into sticks.
2. Serve with hummus for dipping.

Day 3:

Breakfast: Green Smoothie

Ingredients:
- 1 ripe banana
- 1 cup spinach
- ½ cup chopped pineapple

- ½ cup almond milk (or other plant-based milk)

- 1 tablespoon chia seeds

Preparation:

1. Combine the banana, spinach, pineapple, almond milk, and chia seeds in a blender.

2. Blend until smooth and creamy.

3. Turn into a glass and enjoy this refreshing and nutrient-packed green smoothie.

Lunch: Quinoa Stuffed Bell Peppers

Ingredients:

- 2 bell peppers (any color)

- ½ cup cooked quinoa

- ¼ cup black beans, rinsed and drained

- ¼ cup corn kernels

- ¼ cup diced tomatoes

- 2 tablespoons diced red onion

- 1 tablespoon chopped fresh cilantro

- Juice of 1 lime

- Salt and pepper to taste

Preparation:

1. Heat oven to 375 degrees Fahrenheit (190 degrees Celsius).

2. Remove the bell peppers' tops, seeds, and membranes.

3. Combine cooked quinoa, black beans, corn kernels, diced tomatoes, red onion, cilantro, lime juice, salt, and pepper in a bowl.

4. Fill the bell peppers with the mixture and place them in a baking dish.

5. Bake for 25-30 minutes until the bell peppers are tender and slightly charred.

6. Serve the quinoa stuffed bell peppers as a wholesome and flavorful lunch option.

Dinner: Baked Lemon Herb Chicken with Steamed Broccoli and Brown Rice

Ingredients:

- 4 ounces chicken breast

- Juice of 1 lemon

- 1 teaspoon dried herbs (thyme, rosemary, oregano, for example)

- Salt and pepper to taste
- 1 cup steamed broccoli florets
- ½ cup cooked brown rice

Preparation:

1. Heat oven to 375 degrees Fahrenheit (190 degrees Celsius).
2. Place the chicken breast on a baking sheet with parchment paper.
3. Squeeze lemon juice over the chicken and sprinkle with dried herbs, salt, and pepper.
4. Bake for 20-25 minutes until the chicken is cooked and golden brown.
5. Serve the baked lemon herb chicken with steamed broccoli and a side of cooked brown rice for a nourishing and satisfying dinner.

Snack: Apple Slices with Almond Butter

Ingredients:

- 1 apple, sliced
- 2 tablespoons almond butter

Preparation:

1. Slice the apple into thin wedges.

2. Spread almond butter onto each apple slice.

3. Enjoy this delicious and healthy snack combination.

Day 4:

Breakfast: Overnight Chia Pudding

Ingredients:

- 2 tablespoons chia seeds

- ½ cup almond milk (or plant-based milk of choice)

- 1 tablespoon maple syrup or honey

- ¼ teaspoon vanilla extract

- Toppings of choice (such as fresh berries, sliced banana, or chopped nuts)

Preparation:

1. Combine chia seeds, almond milk, maple syrup or honey, and vanilla extract in a jar or bowl.

2. Stir well to ensure the chia seeds are evenly distributed and not clumping together.

3. Refrigerate for at least 4 hours or overnight to allow the chia seeds to absorb the liquid and thicken.

4. In the morning, give the chia pudding a good stir. If desired, add a splash of additional almond milk for desired consistency.

5. Top with your favorite toppings, such as fresh berries, sliced bananas, or chopped nuts.

Lunch: Mediterranean Quinoa Salad

Ingredients:

- ½ cup cooked quinoa

- ½ cup chopped cucumber

- ½ cup halved cherry tomatoes

- ¼ cup sliced Kalamata olives

- 2 tablespoons crumbled feta cheese

- 2 tablespoons chopped fresh parsley

- 1 tablespoon lemon juice

- 1 tablespoon extra-virgin olive oil

- Salt and pepper to taste

Preparation:

1. Combine cooked quinoa, chopped cucumber, cherry tomatoes, Kalamata olives, feta cheese, and fresh parsley in a bowl.

2. To make the dressing, combine lemon juice, olive oil, salt, and pepper in a separate small bowl.

3. Drizzle the dressing over the quinoa salad and toss gently to coat all the ingredients.

4. Allow the salad to sit for a few minutes to allow the flavors to meld together.

5. Serve this refreshing and satisfying Mediterranean quinoa salad for a nutritious lunch.

Dinner: Baked Salmon with Roasted Vegetables

Ingredients:

- 4 ounces salmon fillet
- ½ tablespoon olive oil
- ½ teaspoon dried dill
- ¼ teaspoon garlic powder
- Salt and pepper to taste
- 1 cup mixed roasted vegetables (such as broccoli, carrots, and Brussels sprouts)

- Lemon wedges for serving

Preparation:

1. Heat oven to 375 degrees Fahrenheit (190 degrees Celsius).

2. Place the salmon fillet on a parchment-lined baking sheet.

3. Drizzle the salmon with olive oil and sprinkle with dried dill, garlic powder, salt, and pepper.

4. Bake for 12-15 minutes until the salmon is cooked and flakes easily with a fork.

5. While baking the salmon, toss the mixed vegetables with olive oil, salt, and pepper on a separate baking sheet.

6. Roast the vegetables in the oven for 20-25 minutes until tender and slightly caramelized.

7. Serve the baked salmon with roasted vegetables and lemon wedges for a well-balanced and satisfying dinner.

Snack: Greek Yogurt with Berries and Almonds

Ingredients:

- ½ cup plain Greek yogurt

- ¼ cup mixed berries (such as strawberries, blueberries, and raspberries)

- 1 tablespoon chopped almonds

Preparation:

1. In a bowl, spoon Greek yogurt.

2. Top with mixed berries and chopped almonds.

3. Enjoy this protein-packed and antioxidant-rich snack.

Day 5:

Breakfast: Veggie Omelette

Ingredients:

- 2 eggs
- ¼ cup diced bell peppers (any color)
- ¼ cup diced onion
- ¼ cup sliced mushrooms
- Handful of spinach leaves
- Salt and pepper to taste
- 1 teaspoon olive oil

Preparation:

1. Whisk the eggs together with salt and pepper in a bowl.

2. Warm olive oil in a non-stick skillet over medium heat.

3. Add the diced bell peppers, onion, and mushrooms to the skillet. Sauté until they are slightly softened.

4. Add the spinach leaves and cook until they wilt.

5. Pour the whisked eggs over the vegetables in the skillet, and spread them evenly.

6. Allow the omelet to cook for a few minutes until the bottom is set.

7. Gently flip the omelet to cook the other side for another minute.

8. Transfer the veggie omelet to a plate and serve hot.

Lunch: Lentil and Vegetable Soup

Ingredients:

- ½ cup dried lentils, rinsed

- 1 tablespoon olive oil

- ½ cup diced carrots

- ½ cup diced celery

- ½ cup diced onion

- 2 garlic cloves, minced

- 4 cups vegetable broth

- 1 teaspoon dried thyme

- ½ teaspoon cumin

- Salt and pepper to taste

- Fresh parsley for garnish

Preparation:

1. In a saucepan over medium heat, warm the olive oil.

2. Add diced carrots, celery, onion, and minced garlic to the pot. Cook the vegetables until they are just tender.

3. Add the dried lentils, vegetable broth, thyme, and cumin to the pot.

4. Bring the mixture to a boil, then reduce the heat to low and simmer for about 25-30 minutes or until the lentils are cooked and tender.

5. Season with salt and pepper as desired.

6. Ladle the lentil and vegetable soup into bowls, garnish with fresh parsley, and serve.

Dinner: Grilled chicken breast with roasted sweet potatoes and broccoli steamed

Ingredients:

- 4 ounces chicken breast

- 1 tablespoon olive oil

- ½ teaspoon paprika

- ¼ teaspoon garlic powder

- Salt and pepper to taste

- 1 small sweet potato, cubed

- 1 cup broccoli florets

Preparation:

1. Heat the grill or grill pan to medium-high temperature.

2. Add olive oil, paprika, garlic powder, salt, and pepper in a bowl.

3. Brush the chicken breast with the spice mixture on both sides.

4. Grill the chicken breast for 6-8 minutes per side or until cooked through.

5. While the chicken is grilling, preheat the oven to 425°F (220°C).

6. Toss the cubed sweet potatoes with olive oil, salt, and pepper, then spread on a baking sheet.

7. Roast the sweet potatoes in the oven for 20-25 minutes or until tender and slightly caramelized.

8. Steam the broccoli florets until they are crisp-tender.

9. Serve the grilled chicken breast with roasted sweet potatoes and steamed broccoli.

Snack: Carrot Sticks with Hummus

Ingredients:
- 1 medium carrot, cut into sticks
- 2 tablespoons hummus

Preparation:
1. Cut the carrot into sticks.
2. Serve the carrot sticks with hummus for a crunchy and satisfying snack.

Day 6:

Breakfast: Blueberry Overnight Oats

Ingredients:
- ½ cup rolled oats
- ½ cup almond milk
- ½ cup Greek yogurt
- 1 tablespoon chia seeds
- ½ teaspoon vanilla extract
- ¼ cup fresh or frozen blueberries

- 1 tablespoon honey (optional)

Preparation:

1. Combine rolled oats, almond milk, Greek yogurt, chia seeds, and vanilla extract in a jar or container.
2. Stir well to ensure all ingredients are mixed.
3. Gently fold in the blueberries.
4. Cover the jar or container and refrigerate overnight.
5. In the morning, stir the oats well and add honey if desired.
6. Enjoy your delicious and nutritious blueberry overnight oats!

Lunch: Quinoa Salad with Roasted Vegetables

Ingredients:

- ½ cup cooked quinoa
- 1 cup mixed roasted vegetables (such as bell peppers, zucchini, and eggplant)
- 2 cups mixed salad greens
- ¼ cup crumbled feta cheese
- 2 tablespoons balsamic vinaigrette

Preparation:

1. Cook quinoa according to package guide and let it cool.

2. Heat oven to 400°F (200°C).

3. Toss the mixed vegetables with olive oil, salt, and pepper, then spread on a baking sheet.

4. Roast the vegetables in the oven for about 20-25 minutes or until tender and lightly caramelized.

5. Combine cooked quinoa, roasted vegetables, mixed salad greens, and crumbled feta cheese in a salad bowl.

6. Drizzle balsamic vinaigrette over the salad and toss gently to coat.

7. Serve the quinoa salad as a hearty and nutritious lunch option.

Dinner: Salmon Baked with Quinoa and Steamed Asparagus

Ingredients:

- 4 ounces salmon fillet

- 1 tablespoon olive oil

- ½ teaspoon dried dill

- Salt and pepper to taste

- ½ cup cooked quinoa

- Steamed asparagus spears

Preparation:

1. Heat oven to 375 degrees Fahrenheit (190 degrees Celsius).
2. Place the salmon fillet on a parchment-lined baking sheet.
3. Drizzle olive oil over the salmon and sprinkle with dried dill, salt, and pepper.
4. Bake the salmon for 15-20 minutes or until it flakes easily with a fork.
5. Prepare the quinoa according to package directions while the salmon bakes.
6. Steam the asparagus spears until they are tender-crisp.
7. Serve the baked salmon with cooked quinoa and steamed asparagus for a wholesome and satisfying dinner.

Snack: Apple Slices with Almond Butter

Ingredients:

- 1 medium apple, sliced
- 1 tablespoon almond butter

Preparation:

1. Slice the apple into thin wedges.

2. On each apple slice, spread almond butter.

3. Enjoy the sweet and nutty flavors as a delicious and nourishing snack.

Day 7:

Breakfast: Veggie Omelette

Ingredients:

- 2 eggs
- ¼ cup diced bell peppers
- ¼ cup diced tomatoes
- ¼ cup diced spinach
- 2 tablespoons diced onions
- Salt and pepper to taste
- 1 teaspoon olive oil

Preparation:

1. Whisk the eggs with salt and pepper in a mixing bowl.

2. Warm olive oil in a non-stick skillet over medium heat.

3. Add the diced bell peppers, tomatoes, spinach, and onions to the skillet.

4. Sauté the vegetables for about 2-3 minutes until they are slightly softened.

5. Pour the whisked eggs over the sautéed vegetables in the skillet.

6. Allow the eggs to cook for a few minutes until they start to set.

7. Gently fold the omelet in half and continue cooking for another minute or until the eggs are fully cooked.

8. Serve the omelet immediately on a plate.

Lunch: Mediterranean Chickpea Salad

Ingredients:

- 1 can chickpeas, drained and rinsed
- 1 cup diced cucumbers
- 1 cup diced tomatoes
- ½ cup diced red onions
- ½ cup chopped fresh parsley
- ¼ cup crumbled feta cheese
- Juice of 1 lemon
- 2 tablespoons extra-virgin olive oil

- Salt and pepper to taste

Preparation:

1. Combine chickpeas, cucumbers, tomatoes, red onions, parsley, and feta cheese in a large bowl.

2. Whisk together lemon juice, olive oil, salt, and pepper in a neat bowl to make the dressing.

3. Pour the dressing over the salad and toss well to coat all the ingredients.

4. Let the salad marinate in the refrigerator for at least 30 minutes before serving.

5. Enjoy the refreshing and flavorful Mediterranean chickpea salad.

Dinner: Grilled chicken breast with roasted sweet potatoes and broccoli steamed

Ingredients:

- 4 ounces boneless, skinless chicken breast

- 1 teaspoon olive oil

- ½ teaspoon dried rosemary

- Salt and pepper to taste

- 1 medium sweet potato, cubed

- Steamed broccoli florets

Preparation:

1. Heat the grill or grill pan on medium-high.

2. Rub the chicken breast with olive oil, dried rosemary, salt, and pepper.

3. Grill the chicken for 6-8 minutes per side until it reaches an internal temperature of 165°F (74°C).

4. While the chicken is grilling, preheat the oven to 425°F (220°C).

5. Toss the sweet potato cubes with olive oil, salt, and pepper, then spread on a baking sheet.

6. Roast the sweet potatoes in the oven for about 20-25 minutes or until they are tender and slightly caramelized.

7. Steam the broccoli florets until they are tender-crisp.

8. Serve the grilled chicken breast with roasted sweet potatoes and steamed broccoli for a satisfying and nutritious dinner.

Snack: Greek Yogurt with Berries

Ingredients:

- ½ cup Greek yogurt

- ¼ cup mixed berries (such as blueberries, strawberries, and raspberries)

- 1 tablespoon honey (optional)

Preparation:

1. Fill a bowl halfway with Greek yogurt.

2. Top it with mixed berries and drizzle honey over the yogurt if desired.

3. Enjoy the creamy and tangy Greek yogurt with the natural sweetness of the berries as a refreshing snack.

Day 8:

Breakfast: Quinoa Breakfast Bowl

Ingredients:

- ½ cup cooked quinoa

- ¼ cup almond milk

- 1 tablespoon chia seeds

- 1 tablespoon maple syrup

- ½ teaspoon vanilla extract

- ¼ cup sliced almonds

- ½ cup mixed berries (such as blueberries and raspberries)

Preparation:

1. Combine cooked quinoa, almond milk, chia seeds, maple syrup, and vanilla extract in a bowl.

2. Stir well to ensure the ingredients are fully combined.

3. Let the mixture sit for 5-10 minutes to let the chia seeds thicken.

4. Top the quinoa mixture with sliced almonds and mixed berries.

5. Enjoy this nutritious and satisfying quinoa breakfast bowl.

Lunch: Lentil and Vegetable Soup

Ingredients:

- ½ cup dried green lentils, rinsed

- 4 cups vegetable broth

- 1 tablespoon olive oil

- 1 small onion, diced

- 2 cloves garlic, minced

- 1 carrot, diced

- 1 celery stalk, diced

- 1 zucchini, diced

- 1 teaspoon dried thyme

- ½ teaspoon ground cumin

- Salt and pepper to taste

- Fresh parsley, chopped (for garnish)

Preparation:

1. Warm olive oil in a large neat pot over medium heat.

2. Sauté the diced onion and minced garlic in the pot until fragrant and translucent.

3. Add diced carrot, celery, and zucchini to the pot and cook for a few minutes until they soften.

4. Stir in dried thyme and ground cumin, and season with salt and pepper.

5. Add rinsed lentils and vegetable broth to the pot, and bring the mixture to a boil.

6. Reduce the heat and simmer for about 20-25 minutes or until the lentils are tender.

7. Adjust the seasoning if needed.

8. Serve the lentil and vegetable soup hot, garnished with fresh parsley.

Dinner: Baked Salmon with Quinoa and Steamed Broccoli

Ingredients:

- 4 ounces salmon fillet
- 1 teaspoon olive oil
- Lemon slices
- Salt and pepper to taste
- ½ cup cooked quinoa
- Steamed broccoli florets

Preparation:

1. Heat oven to 375 degrees Fahrenheit (190 degrees Celsius).

2. Place the salmon fillet on a parchment-lined baking sheet.

3. Drizzle the salmon with olive oil and season with salt, pepper, and lemon slices.

4. Bake the salmon in the oven for about 12-15 minutes or until it is cooked.

5. While baking the salmon, reheat the cooked quinoa and steam the broccoli florets.

6. Serve the baked salmon with quinoa and steamed broccoli for a nutritious and flavorful dinner.

Snack: Carrot Sticks with Hummus

Ingredients:

- 1 large carrot, cut into sticks
- 2 tablespoons hummus

Preparation:

1. Wash and peel the carrot, then cut it into sticks.
2. Serve the carrot sticks with hummus for a crunchy and satisfying snack.

Day 10:

Breakfast: Oatmeal with Berries and Almonds

Ingredients:

- ½ cup rolled oats
- 1 cup unsweetened almond milk
- 1 tablespoon chia seeds
- Berries (blueberries and raspberries, for example)
- 1 tablespoon sliced almonds

Preparation:

1. In a saucepan, combine rolled oats and almond milk.

2. Cook over medium heat, stirring occasionally, until the oats have absorbed the liquid and reached your desired consistency.

3. Take the pan off the heat and stir the chia seeds.

4. Transfer the oatmeal to a bowl.

5. Top with mixed berries and sliced almonds.

6. Enjoy this hearty and nutritious breakfast to start your day.

Lunch: Chickpea Salad Wraps

Ingredients:

- 1 cup rinsed and drained canned chickpeas
- ¼ cup diced cucumber
- ¼ cup diced tomato
- 2 tablespoons diced red onion
- 2 tablespoons chopped fresh parsley
- Juice of 1 lemon
- 1 tablespoon extra virgin olive oil
- Salt and pepper to taste
- Whole grain tortillas
- Baby spinach or lettuce leaves

Preparation:

1. Combine chickpeas, cucumber, tomato, red onion, and parsley in a bowl.

2. Whisk together lemon juice, olive oil, salt, and pepper in a small bowl to make the dressing.

3. Toss the chickpea mixture with the dressing to combine.

4. Warm the whole grain tortillas in a skillet or microwave.

5. Spread a layer of baby spinach or lettuce leaves on each tortilla.

6. Spoon the chickpea salad onto the tortillas.

7. Wrap the tortillas tightly, cut them in half if desired, and enjoy these flavorful and satisfying wraps for lunch.

Dinner: Baked Salmon with Quinoa and Steamed Broccoli

Ingredients:

- 4 ounces salmon fillet
- 1 teaspoon lemon juice
- ½ teaspoon dried dill
- Salt and pepper to taste
- ½ cup cooked quinoa
- Steamed broccoli (as a side dish)

Preparation:

1. Heat oven to 375 degrees Fahrenheit (190 degrees Celsius).

2. Place the salmon fillet on a parchment-lined baking sheet.

3. Drizzle the salmon with lemon juice and sprinkle with dried dill, salt, and pepper.

4. Bake the salmon in the oven for about 12-15 minutes or until it flakes easily with a fork.

5. While the salmon is baking, reheat the cooked quinoa.

6. Serve the baked salmon with quinoa and steamed broccoli for a nutritious and delicious dinner.

Snack: Carrot Sticks with Hummus

Ingredients:

- Carrot sticks

- Hummus (store-bought or homemade)

Preparation:

1. Wash and peel carrots, and cut them into sticks.

2. Serve the carrot sticks with hummus for a crunchy and satisfying snack.

Day 11:

Breakfast: Greek Yogurt Parfait

Ingredients:

- ½ cup plain Greek yogurt
- ¼ cup granola (look for a low-sugar option)
- Berries (strawberries and blueberries, for example)
- 1 tablespoon honey (optional)

Preparation:

1. Get the Greek yogurt, granola, and mixed berries in a bowl or glass.
2. Drizzle with honey, if desired, for added sweetness.
3. Enjoy this creamy and nutritious parfait to start your day on a refreshing note.

Lunch: Quinoa Salad with Avocado and Black Beans

Ingredients:

- ½ cup cooked quinoa
- ½ avocado, diced
- ¼ cup canned black beans, rinsed and drained

- 2 tablespoons chopped fresh cilantro
- Juice of 1 lime
- 1 tablespoon extra virgin olive oil
- Salt and pepper to taste
- Greens (e.g., baby spinach or arugula)

Preparation:

1. Mix cooked quinoa, diced avocado, black beans, and cilantro.

2. Whisk together lime juice, olive oil, salt, and pepper in a neat bowl to make the dressing.

3. Pour the dressing over the quinoa mixture and toss to combine.

4. Serve the quinoa salad on a bed of mixed greens for a satisfying and protein-packed lunch.

Dinner: Grilled Chicken Breast with Roasted Vegetables

Ingredients:

- 4 ounces chicken breast
- 1 teaspoon olive oil
- ½ teaspoon dried rosemary
- Salt and pepper to taste

- Vegetables (including bell peppers, zucchini, and cherry tomatoes)
- 1 tablespoon balsamic vinegar

Preparation:

1. Preheat the grill or grill pan.
2. Rub the chicken breast with olive oil and sprinkle with dried rosemary, salt, and pepper.
3. Grill the chicken breast for 6-8 minutes per side or until cooked through.
4. While the chicken is grilling, preheat the oven to 400°F (200°C).
5. Toss the assorted vegetables with olive oil, salt, and pepper on a baking sheet.
6. Roast the vegetables in the oven for 15-20 minutes or until tender.
7. Drizzle the roasted vegetables with balsamic vinegar for added flavor.
8. Serve the grilled chicken breast with roasted vegetables for a nutritious and satisfying dinner.

Snack: Apple Slices with Almond Butter

Ingredients:

- Apple, sliced
- Almond butter (look for a natural, unsweetened option)

Preparation:

1. Slice the apple into thin wedges.
2. On each apple slice, spread almond butter.
3. Enjoy the crisp and creamy combination of apple and almond butter as a delicious snack.

Day 12:

Breakfast: Veggie Scramble

Ingredients:

- 2 eggs
- 1 tablespoon olive oil
- ¼ cup diced bell peppers
- ¼ cup diced onion
- ½ cup spinach leaves
- Salt and pepper to taste
- Whole grain toast (optional)

Preparation:

1. In a neat bowl, whisk the eggs until well beaten.

2. In a skillet over medium heat, heat the olive oil.

3. Add diced bell peppers and onions to the skillet and sauté until softened.

4. Add spinach leaves to the skillet and cook until wilted.

5. Pour the beaten eggs into the skillet and cook, stirring occasionally, until fully cooked and scrambled.

6. To taste, season with salt and pepper.

7. Serve the veggie scramble with whole grain toast, if desired, for a satisfying and protein-rich breakfast.

Lunch: Quinoa Stuffed Bell Peppers

Ingredients:

- 2 bell peppers

- ½ cup cooked quinoa

- ¼ cup black beans, rinsed and drained

- ¼ cup diced tomatoes

- 2 tablespoons chopped fresh parsley

- 1 tablespoon lemon juice

- 1 tablespoon olive oil

- Salt and pepper to taste

Preparation:

1. Heat oven to 375 degrees Fahrenheit (190 degrees Celsius).

2. Remove the bell peppers' tops, seeds, and membranes.

3. Combine cooked quinoa, black beans, diced tomatoes, parsley, lemon juice, olive oil, salt, and pepper in a bowl.

4. Spoon the quinoa mixture into the hollowed-out bell peppers.

5. Place the stuffed bell peppers on a baking sheet and bake in the oven for about 20-25 minutes or until the peppers are tender.

6. Remove from the oven and let them cool for a few minutes before serving.

7. Enjoy the flavorful and nutritious quinoa stuffed bell peppers for a satisfying lunch.

Dinner: Baked Cod with Roasted Asparagus

Ingredients:

- 4 ounces cod fillet

- 1 teaspoon lemon juice

- 1 teaspoon olive oil

- ½ teaspoon dried dill

- Salt and pepper to taste

- Asparagus spears

- 1 tablespoon grated Parmesan cheese (optional)

Preparation:

1. Heat oven to 375 degrees Fahrenheit (190 degrees Celsius).

2. Place the cod fillet on a baking sheet with parchment paper.

3. Drizzle the cod with lemon juice and olive oil.

4. Sprinkle dried dill, salt, and pepper over the cod.

5. Bake the cod in the preheated oven for about 12-15 minutes or until it flakes easily with a fork.

6. While the cod is baking, prepare the asparagus by trimming the woody ends and tossing them with olive oil, salt, and pepper.

7. Place the asparagus on a separate baking sheet and roast in the oven for 10-12 minutes or until tender.

8. Optional: Sprinkle-grated Parmesan cheese over the roasted asparagus for added flavor.

9. Serve the baked cod with roasted asparagus for a delicious, heart-healthy dinner.

Snack: Mixed Nuts and Seeds

Ingredients:

- Assorted nuts and seeds (such as almonds, walnuts, pumpkin seeds, and sunflower seeds)

Preparation:

1. Combine the mixed nuts and seeds in a small container or snack bag.
2. Enjoy a handful of this nutritious snack between meals.

Day 13:

Breakfast: Berry Oatmeal

Ingredients:

- ½ cup rolled oats
- 1 cup unsweetened almond milk
- ¼ cup mixed berries (such as blueberries, raspberries, and strawberries)
- 1 tablespoon chia seeds
- 1 tablespoon maple syrup (optional)
- 1 teaspoon chopped nuts (almonds or walnuts)

Preparation:

1. In a saucepan, combine rolled oats and almond milk.

2. Cook over medium heat, stirring occasionally, until the oats are tender and the mixture thickens.

3. Remove from heat and stir the mixed berries and chia seeds.

4. Sweeten with maple syrup, if desired.

5. Top with chopped nuts for added crunch and protein.

6. Enjoy the nourishing and satisfying berry oatmeal to start your day.

Lunch: Chickpea Salad Wrap

Ingredients:

- ½ cup rinsed and drained chickpeas (canned)

- ¼ cup diced cucumber

- ¼ cup diced bell peppers

- 2 tablespoons diced red onion

- 2 tablespoons chopped fresh parsley

- 1 tablespoon lemon juice

- 1 tablespoon olive oil

- Salt and pepper to taste

- Whole grain tortilla or wrap

Preparation:

1. Mix a bowl of chickpeas, cucumber, bell peppers, red onion, parsley, lemon juice, olive oil, salt, and pepper.

2. Mash the chickpeas slightly with a fork to create a chunky texture.

3. Warm the whole grain tortilla or wrap it slightly to make it more pliable.

4. Spoon the chickpea salad onto the tortilla and wrap it tightly.

5. If needed, Cut the wrap in half and secure it with toothpicks.

6. Enjoy the flavorful and fiber-rich chickpea salad wrap for a wholesome lunch.

Dinner: Grilled Chicken with Roasted Vegetables

Ingredients:

- 4 ounces chicken breast
- 1 tablespoon lemon juice
- 1 tablespoon olive oil
- ½ teaspoon dried herbs (such as thyme or rosemary)
- Salt and pepper to taste

- Assorted vegetables (such as bell peppers, zucchini, and eggplant)

- 1 tablespoon balsamic vinegar (optional)

Preparation:

1. Preheat the grill or grill pan.

2. Combine lemon juice, olive oil, dried herbs, salt, and pepper in a bowl.

3. Coat the chicken breast with the marinade and let it sit for a few minutes.

4. Grill the chicken breast for 6-8 minutes per side or until cooked through.

5. While the chicken grills, prepare the vegetables by slicing them into desired shapes.

6. Toss the vegetables with olive oil, salt, and pepper.

7. Drizzle balsamic vinegar over the vegetables for added flavor if desired.

8. Roast the vegetables in the oven at 400°F (200°C) for about 20-25 minutes or until tender.

9. Serve the grilled chicken with a side of roasted vegetables for a protein-packed and nutrient-rich dinner.

Snack: Apple Slices with Nut Butter

Ingredients:

- 1 medium apple, sliced

- 1 tablespoon nut butter (almond or peanut butter preferred)

Preparation:

1. Slice the apple into thin wedges or rounds.

2. Spread nut butter on each apple slice.

3. Enjoy the crisp, satisfying apple slices with a creamy nut butter dip.

Day 14:

Breakfast: Veggie Scramble

Ingredients:

- 2 eggs

- ½ cup chopped mixed vegetables (such as bell peppers, spinach, and onions)

- 1 tablespoon olive oil

- Salt and pepper to taste

Preparation:

1. In a bowl, whisk the eggs until well beaten.

2. Heat olive oil in a non-stick skillet over medium heat.

3. Add the chopped vegetables to the skillet and sauté until they soften.

4. Pour the beaten eggs over the vegetables and scramble them until cooked.

5. Season to taste with salt and pepper.

6. Enjoy the protein-rich veggie scramble to kick-start your day.

Lunch: Quinoa Salad

Ingredients:

- ½ cup cooked quinoa
- ¼ cup diced cucumber
- ¼ cup cherry tomatoes, halved
- 2 tbsp. chopped fresh herbs (parsley, basil, etc.)
- 1 tablespoon lemon juice
- 1 tablespoon extra virgin olive oil
- Salt and pepper to taste

Preparation:

1. Combine cooked quinoa, diced cucumber, cherry tomatoes, and chopped herbs in a bowl.

2. Whisk together lemon juice, olive oil, salt, and pepper in a separate small bowl to make the dressing.

3. Toss the quinoa salad with the dressing to combine.

4. Adjust the seasoning if needed.

5. Enjoy the refreshing and nutritious quinoa salad for a light and satisfying lunch.

Dinner: Baked Salmon with Steamed Vegetables

Ingredients:

- 4 ounces salmon fillet
- 1 tablespoon lemon juice
- 1 tablespoon extra virgin olive oil
- ½ teaspoon dried dill
- Salt and pepper to taste
- Steamed vegetables (including broccoli, carrots, and cauliflower)

Preparation:

1. Heat oven to 400°F (200°C).

2. Place the salmon fillet on a parchment-lined baking sheet.

3. Drizzle lemon juice and olive oil over the salmon.

4. Sprinkle dried dill, salt, and pepper evenly on top.

5. Bake the salmon for 12-15 minutes or until cooked to your desired level.

6. While the salmon is baking, steam the vegetables until tender.

7. Serve the baked salmon with steamed vegetables for a heart-healthy and nourishing dinner.

Snack: Greek Yogurt with Berries

Ingredients:

- ½ cup plain Greek yogurt
- ¼ cup mixed berries (such as blueberries, raspberries, and strawberries)
- 1 tablespoon honey (optional)

Preparation:

1. In a bowl, scoop the Greek yogurt.

2. Top the yogurt with mixed berries.

3. Drizzle honey over the yogurt and berries for added sweetness, if desired.

4. Enjoy the creamy and antioxidant-rich Greek yogurt with a burst of fresh berries.

Day 15:

Breakfast: Oatmeal with Almond Butter and Banana

Ingredients:

- ½ cup rolled oats
- 1 cup almond milk
- 1 tablespoon almond butter
- ½ ripe banana, sliced
- 1 tablespoon chopped almonds (optional)

Preparation:

1. Bring the almond milk to a boil in a saucepan.

2. Reduce the heat to low and add the rolled oats. Cook for about 5 minutes until the oats are tender and the mixture thickens, stirring occasionally.

3. Remove from heat and transfer the oatmeal to a bowl.

4. Top with almond butter, sliced banana, and chopped almonds if desired.

5. Enjoy the warm and satisfying oatmeal breakfast to fuel your day.

Lunch: Chickpea Salad Wraps

Ingredients:

- 1 cup cooked chickpeas
- ¼ cup diced bell peppers
- ¼ cup diced cucumber
- 2 tablespoons diced red onion
- 2 tablespoons chopped fresh parsley
- 1 tablespoon lemon juice
- 1 tablespoon extra virgin olive oil
- Salt and pepper to taste
- Whole grain tortilla wraps

Preparation:

1. Combine the cooked chickpeas, diced bell peppers, cucumber, red onion, and parsley in a bowl.

2. Whisk together lemon juice, olive oil, salt, and pepper in a separate small bowl to make the dressing.

3. Toss the chickpea mixture with the dressing to coat.

4. Warm the whole-grain tortilla wraps according to package instructions.

5. Spoon the chickpea salad onto the wraps and roll them up.

6. Serve the chickpea salad wraps as a delicious and protein-packed lunch.

Dinner: Lentil Curry with Brown Rice

Ingredients:

- 1 cup cooked brown lentils
- ½ cup diced tomatoes
- ½ cup diced onion
- 2 cloves garlic, minced
- 1 tablespoon curry powder
- 1 teaspoon ground cumin
- 1 teaspoon ground coriander
- ½ teaspoon turmeric powder
- ½ teaspoon paprika
- 1 cup vegetable broth
- 1 tablespoon olive oil
- Salt and pepper to taste
- Cooked brown rice (for serving)

Preparation:

1. Warm olive oil in a large skillet over medium heat.

2. To the skillet, add the diced onion and minced garlic. Cook until the onion is translucent.

3. Add the diced tomatoes and spices (curry powder, cumin, coriander, turmeric, paprika) to the skillet. Allow the flavors to blend for a minute.

4. Stir in the cooked brown lentils and vegetable broth. Simmer for 10-15 minutes to allow the flavors to blend and the lentils to absorb the sauce.

5. Season to taste with salt and pepper.

6. Serve the lentil curry over cooked brown rice for a hearty and nutritious dinner.

Snack: Carrot Sticks with Hummus

Ingredients:

- 1 medium carrot, cut into sticks
- 2 tablespoons hummus

Preparation:

1. Wash and peel the carrot. Cut it into sticks.

2. Serve the carrot sticks with hummus for a crunchy and satisfying snack.

Day 16:

Breakfast: Green Smoothie Bowl

Ingredients:
- 1 ripe banana
- 1 cup spinach
- ½ cup frozen mango chunks
- ½ cup unsweetened almond milk
- Toppings: sliced strawberries, chia seeds, granola

Preparation:
1. Combine the ripe banana, spinach, frozen mango chunks, and almond milk in a blender.
2. Blend until smooth and creamy.
3. Fill a bowl halfway with the green smoothie.
4. Top with sliced strawberries, chia seeds, and granola for added texture and flavor.
5. Enjoy the refreshing and nutritious green smoothie bowl.

Lunch: Quinoa Salad with Roasted Vegetables

Ingredients:

- ½ cup cooked quinoa
- 1 cup mixed roasted vegetables (such as bell peppers, zucchini, and eggplant)
- 2 cups mixed greens
- ¼ cup crumbled feta cheese (optional)
- 2 tablespoons balsamic vinaigrette

Preparation:

1. Cook quinoa according to package instructions and let it cool.
2. Preheat the oven to 400°F (200°C).
3. Toss the mixed vegetables with olive oil, salt, and pepper.
4. Spread the vegetables on a baking sheet and roast for 15-20 minutes until tender.
5. Combine the cooked quinoa, roasted vegetables, mixed greens, and crumbled feta cheese in a bowl.
6. Drizzle with balsamic vinaigrette and toss to coat.
7. Enjoy the flavorful and nutritious quinoa salad for lunch.

Dinner: Baked Salmon with Roasted Asparagus

Ingredients:

- 1 salmon fillet
- 1 tablespoon lemon juice
- 1 tablespoon extra virgin olive oil
- Salt and pepper to taste
- 8-10 asparagus spears, trimmed
- 1 tablespoon balsamic glaze (optional)

Preparation:

1. Preheat the oven to 400°F (200°C).

2. Place the salmon fillet on a parchment-lined baking sheet.

3. Drizzle the salmon with lemon juice and olive oil.

4. Season with salt and pepper.

5. Arrange the trimmed asparagus spears around the salmon on the baking sheet.

6. Roast in the oven for 12-15 minutes until the salmon is cooked and the asparagus is tender.

7. Remove from the oven and drizzle with balsamic glaze, if desired.

8. Serve the baked salmon with roasted asparagus for a nutritious and satisfying dinner.

Snack: Apple Slices with Almond Butter

Ingredients:

- 1 medium apple, sliced

- 2 tablespoons almond butter

Preparation:

1. Wash and slice the apple into thin wedges.

2. Spread almond butter on the apple slices for a delicious and healthy snack.

Day 17:

Breakfast: Veggie Omelette

Ingredients:

- 2 eggs

- 1 tablespoon chopped bell peppers

- 1 tablespoon chopped onions

- 1 tablespoon chopped spinach

- Salt and pepper to taste

- Cooking spray

Preparation:

1. Mix the eggs in a mixing bowl until well combined.

2. Heat a non-stick skillet over medium heat and coat with cooking spray.

3. Add the chopped bell peppers, onions, and spinach to the skillet and sauté for a few minutes until slightly softened.

4. Pour the beaten eggs over the sautéed vegetables.

5. Cook the omelet until the eggs are set and the edges are golden.

6. To taste as desired, add pepper and salt.

7. Gently fold the omelet in half and transfer it to a plate.

8. Enjoy the nutritious and protein-packed veggie omelet for breakfast.

Lunch: Lentil Soup

Ingredients:

- ½ cup dry lentils, rinsed and drained

- 1 small onion, chopped

- 2 cloves garlic, minced

- 2 carrots, diced

- 2 celery stalks, diced

- 4 cups vegetable broth

- 1 teaspoon cumin

- ½ teaspoon paprika

- Salt and pepper to taste

- Fresh parsley for garnish (optional)

Preparation:

1. Heat a tablespoon of olive oil over medium heat in a large pot.

2. Add the chopped onion and minced garlic to the pot and sauté until fragrant and golden.

3. Add the diced carrots and celery to the pot and continue to cook for a few minutes.

4. Rinse the lentils, then add them to the pot.

5. Pour in the vegetable broth and add the cumin and paprika.

6. Bring the soup to a boil, then reduce the heat to low and simmer for 30-40 minutes until the lentils are tender.

7. Season with salt and pepper to desired taste.

8. If desired, Ladle the lentil soup into bowls and garnish with fresh parsley.

9. Enjoy the comforting and nourishing lentil soup for lunch.

Dinner: Grilled Chicken with Steamed Broccoli

Ingredients:

- 1 chicken breast
- 1 tablespoon olive oil
- Juice of 1 lemon
- Salt and pepper to taste
- 1 cup steamed broccoli florets

Preparation:

1. Preheat the grill to medium-high heat.

2. Add olive oil, lemon juice, salt, and pepper in a bowl.

3. Coat the chicken breast with the marinade.

4. Place the chicken breast on the preheated grill and cook for 6-8 minutes on each side until cooked.

5. Remove the chicken from the grill and allow it rest for a few minutes before slicing.

6. Serve the grilled chicken with steamed broccoli for a healthy and satisfying dinner.

Snack: Greek Yogurt with Berries

Ingredients:

- ½ cup plain Greek yogurt
- ½ cup berries (strawberries, blueberries, and raspberries)
- 1 tablespoon honey (optional)

Preparation:

1. In a bowl, spoon the Greek yogurt.
2. Top with mixed berries and drizzle with honey, if desired.
3. Enjoy creamy and antioxidant-rich Greek yogurt with berries as a nutritious snack.

Day 18:

Breakfast: Overnight Chia Pudding

Ingredients:

- 2 tablespoons chia seeds
- ½ cup unsweetened almond milk
- 1 tablespoon honey or maple syrup
- ½ teaspoon vanilla extract
- Fresh berries for topping

Preparation:

1. Combine the chia seeds, almond milk, honey or maple syrup, and vanilla extract in a jar or bowl.

2. Stir thoroughly to ensure that the chia seeds are evenly distributed.

3. Cover the jar or bowl and refrigerate overnight.

4. In the morning, give the chia pudding a good stir.

5. Top with fresh berries.

6. Enjoy the creamy and nutritious overnight chia pudding for breakfast.

Lunch: Quinoa Salad with Roasted Vegetables

Ingredients:

- ½ cup cooked quinoa

- 1 cup mixed roasted vegetables (such as bell peppers, zucchini, and eggplant)

- Handful of baby spinach leaves

- ¼ cup crumbled feta cheese

- 1 tablespoon extra virgin olive oil

- Juice of 1 lemon

- Salt and pepper to taste

Preparation:

1. Combine the cooked quinoa, roasted vegetables, baby spinach, and crumbled feta cheese in a bowl.

2. Mix the olive oil, lemon juice, salt, and pepper in a separate small bowl to make the dressing.

3. Toss the quinoa salad with the dressing to combine.

4. Adjust the seasoning if needed.

5. Serve the flavorful and nutrient-packed quinoa salad for lunch.

Dinner: Baked Salmon with Asparagus

Ingredients:

- 1 salmon fillet
- 1 tablespoon lemon juice
- 1 teaspoon Dijon mustard
- 1 garlic clove, minced
- Salt and pepper to taste
- 8-10 asparagus spears
- 1 tablespoon olive oil
- Lemon wedges for serving

Preparation:

1. Preheat the oven to 400°F (200°C).

2. Place the salmon fillet on a parchment-lined baking sheet.

3. Mix the lemon juice, Dijon mustard, minced garlic, salt, and pepper in a neat bowl.

4. Spread the mixture evenly over the salmon fillet.

5. Trim the woody ends of the asparagus spears.

6. Place the asparagus on the same baking sheet as the salmon.

7. Drizzle the asparagus with olive oil and season with salt and pepper.

8. Bake in the oven for 12-15 minutes until the salmon is cooked and the asparagus is tender.

9. Serve the baked salmon with roasted asparagus and lemon wedges.

Snack: Almond Butter with Apple Slices

Ingredients:

- 1 tablespoon almond butter
- 1 medium apple, sliced

Preparation:

1. Spread the almond butter on a plate.

2. Serve with apple slices for dipping.

3. Enjoy satisfying and nutrient-rich almond butter with apple slices as a delicious snack.

Day 19:

Breakfast: Veggie Omelette

Ingredients:

- 2 eggs

- ¼ cup diced bell peppers

- ¼ cup diced onions

- ¼ cup chopped spinach

- 2 tablespoons shredded cheddar cheese

- Salt and pepper to taste

- To grease the pan, use cooking spray or olive oil.

Preparation:

1. In a bowl, whisk the eggs together until well beaten.

2. Heat a non-stick skillet over medium heat and lightly grease it with cooking spray or olive oil.

3. Add the diced bell peppers and onions to the skillet and sauté until they soften.

4. Add the chopped spinach to the skillet and cook for another minute until wilted.

5. Pour the beaten eggs into the skillet, ensuring they cover the vegetables evenly.

6. Sprinkle the shredded cheddar cheese on top.

7. Cook the omelet for a few minutes until the edges are set.

8. Carefully flip the omelet over and cook for another minute or until the eggs are fully cooked.

9. Season with salt and pepper as desired to taste.

10. Serve the delicious veggie omelet for a nutritious breakfast.

Lunch: Greek Salad with Grilled Chicken

Ingredients:

- 4 ounces grilled chicken breast, sliced

- 2 cups mixed greens

- ¼ cup cherry tomatoes, halved

- ¼ cup sliced cucumbers

- 2 tablespoons crumbled feta cheese

- 8 Kalamata olives

- 1 tablespoon extra virgin olive oil

- Juice of 1 lemon

- Salt and pepper to taste

Preparation:

1. Combine the mixed greens, cherry tomatoes, sliced cucumbers, crumbled feta cheese, and Kalamata olives in a large bowl.

2. Drizzle the olive oil and lemon juice over the salad.

3. Season with salt and pepper as desired to taste.

4. Toss the salad to coat the ingredients with the dressing.

5. Top the salad with sliced grilled chicken breast.

6. Enjoy the refreshing and protein-packed Greek salad with grilled chicken for lunch.

Dinner: Lentil Curry with Brown Rice

Ingredients:

- ½ cup cooked brown rice

- 1 cup cooked lentils

- 1 small onion, finely chopped

- 2 cloves garlic, minced

- 1 tablespoon curry powder

- 1 teaspoon ground cumin

- 1 teaspoon ground coriander

- ½ teaspoon turmeric powder

- 1 cup canned diced tomatoes

- ½ cup coconut milk

- 1 tablespoon olive oil

- Salt and pepper to taste

- Fresh cilantro for garnish (optional)

Preparation:

1. Warm up the olive oil in a medium saucepan.

2. Add the chopped onion and minced garlic to the pan and sauté until they become translucent.

3. Stir in the curry powder, cumin, coriander, and turmeric powder, and cook for another minute to release the flavors.

4. Add the canned diced tomatoes (including the juice) to the pan and simmer for 5 minutes.

5. Pour in the coconut milk and cooked lentils and season with salt and pepper.

6. Stir well to combine all the ingredients and simmer for 10 minutes.

7. Serve the lentil curry over cooked brown rice.

8. Garnish with fresh cilantro, if desired.

9. Enjoy the delicious, hearty lentil curry with brown rice for dinner.

Snack: Carrot Sticks with Hummus

Ingredients:
- 1 medium carrot, cut into sticks
- 2 tablespoons hummus

Preparation:
1. Arrange the carrot sticks on a plate.
2. Serve with hummus for dipping.
3. Enjoy the crunchy and nutritious carrot sticks with hummus as a satisfying snack.

Day 20:

Breakfast: Blueberry Chia Seed Smoothie

Ingredients:
- 1 cup frozen blueberries
- 1 ripe banana
- 1 tablespoon chia seeds
- 1 cup almond milk (or plant-based milk of choice)

-1 tablespoon honey or maple syrup (optional)

Preparation:

1. In a blender, combine the frozen blueberries, ripe banana, chia seeds, almond milk, and honey or maple syrup (if desired).

2. Blend until smooth and creamy.

3. For breakfast, Pour the smoothie into a glass and enjoy the antioxidant-rich and fiber-packed blueberry chia seed smoothie.

Lunch: Quinoa Salad with Roasted Vegetables

Ingredients:

- ½ cup cooked quinoa
- 1 cup mixed roasted vegetables (such as bell peppers, zucchini, and eggplant)
- 2 cups fresh spinach leaves
- ¼ cup crumbled goat cheese
- 2 tablespoons balsamic vinaigrette dressing

Preparation:

1. Mix the cooked quinoa, roasted vegetables, fresh spinach leaves, and crumbled goat cheese in a bowl.

2. Drizzle the balsamic vinaigrette dressing over the salad.

3. Toss well to coat the ingredients with the dressing.

4. Serve the flavorful and nutrient-rich quinoa salad with roasted vegetables for a satisfying lunch.

Dinner: Baked Salmon with Steamed Broccoli and Quinoa

Ingredients:

- 4 ounces salmon fillet
- 1 cup steamed broccoli florets
- ½ cup cooked quinoa
- 1 tablespoon olive oil
- Juice of 1 lemon
- Salt and pepper to taste

Preparation:

1. Heat oven to 375 degrees Fahrenheit (190 degrees Celsius).

2. Place the salmon fillet on a parchment-lined baking sheet.

3. Drizzle olive oil and lemon juice over the salmon.

4. Season with salt and pepper to taste.

5. Bake the salmon in the oven for 12-15 minutes or until cooked.

6. In the meantime, steam the broccoli florets until tender.

7. Serve the baked salmon alongside steamed broccoli and cooked quinoa.

8. Enjoy the delicious omega-3-rich baked salmon with steamed broccoli and quinoa for dinner.

Snack: Almond Butter and Apple Slices

Ingredients:

- 1 medium apple, sliced
- 2 tablespoons almond butter

Preparation:

1. Arrange the apple slices on a plate.

2. Spread almond butter on each slice.

3. Enjoy the sweet and satisfying almond butter and apple slices as a healthy snack.

Day 21:

Breakfast: Veggie Omelette

Ingredients:

- 2 large eggs
- 1/4 cup chopped bell peppers
- 1/4 cup chopped onions
- 1/4 cup chopped spinach
- 2 tablespoons grated Parmesan cheese
- Salt and pepper to taste
- 1 teaspoon olive oil

Preparation:

1. Mix the eggs in a mixing bowl until well combined.
2. Heat the olive oil in a non-stick skillet over medium heat.
3. Add the chopped bell peppers, onions, and spinach to the skillet and sauté until tender.
4. Pour the beaten eggs over the sautéed vegetables and cook for a few minutes until the edges are set.
5. Sprinkle-grated Parmesan cheese, salt, and pepper on top.
6. Fold the omelet in half and cook for another minute until the cheese is melted.

7. Transfer the veggie omelet to a plate and serve it as a nutritious breakfast.

Lunch: Quinoa and Black Bean Salad

Ingredients:

- 1 cup cooked quinoa
- 1 cup rinsed, drained, and canned black beans
- 1/2 cup cherry tomatoes, halved
- 1/4 cup chopped red onion
- 1/4 cup chopped cilantro
- Juice of 1 lime
- 1 tablespoon olive oil
- Salt and pepper to taste

Preparation:

1. Combine cooked quinoa, black beans, cherry tomatoes, red onion, and cilantro in a large bowl.
2. Whisk together lime juice, olive oil, salt, and pepper in a separate small bowl to make the dressing.
3. Pour the dressing over the quinoa mixture and toss well to combine.

4. Mix the flavors by refrigerating the salad for at least 30 minutes before serving.

5. Serve the refreshing, protein-packed quinoa and black bean salad for a nutritious lunch.

Dinner: Grilled Chicken Breast with Roasted Vegetables

Ingredients:

- 4 ounces chicken breast
- 1 cup mixed roasted vegetables (such as carrots, Brussels sprouts, and cauliflower)
- 1 tablespoon olive oil
- 1 teaspoon dried herbs, either thyme or rosemary
- Salt and pepper to taste

Preparation:

1. Preheat the grill to medium heat.

2. Rub the chicken breast with olive oil, dried herbs, salt, and pepper.

3. Grill the chicken for 6-8 minutes per side until cooked.

4. In the meantime, toss the mixed vegetables with olive oil, salt, and pepper.

5. Spread the vegetables on a baking sheet and roast them in the oven at 400°F (200°C) for about 20-25 minutes until tender and lightly browned.

6. Serve the grilled chicken breast with roasted vegetables for a delicious, protein-rich dinner.

Snack: Greek Yogurt with Berries

Ingredients:

- 1/2 cup Greek yogurt

-1/4 cup mixed berries (strawberries, blueberries, raspberries, etc.)

- 1 tablespoon honey (optional, for sweetness)

Preparation:

1. In a small bowl, spoon the Greek yogurt.

2. Top it with mixed berries.

3. Drizzle honey on top if desired for added sweetness.

4. Enjoy the creamy and antioxidant-packed Greek yogurt with fresh berries as a healthy snack.

Conclusion

As you reach the end of the 21-Day Meal Plan for Coronary Health, it's time to reflect on the incredible journey you've undertaken. Over the past three weeks, you've embraced a heart-healthy lifestyle, nourished your body with wholesome ingredients, and prioritized your cardiovascular well-being. Congratulations on this remarkable achievement!

Throughout this meal plan, you've discovered the power of nutrition in reversing coronary artery disease and promoting a healthy heart. By incorporating heart-healthy recipes into your daily life, you've experienced the joy of delicious meals and reaped their numerous health benefits.

Focusing on key nutrients such as omega-3 fatty acids, fiber, antioxidants, and phytochemicals nourishes your body with the essential components to reduce inflammation, improve blood flow, and support optimal heart function. Each recipe was carefully designed to provide diverse flavors, textures, and nutrients, ensuring that your meals were enjoyable and beneficial to your overall health.

But this meal plan is just the beginning of your journey towards lasting coronary health. As you move forward, remember that the habits and practices you've developed over these 21 days are meant to be sustained for the long term. Continue to prioritize your cardiovascular well-being by making mindful choices daily.

Adopt a diet high in fruits, vegetables, whole grains, lean proteins, and healthy fats. Seek out new recipes and flavors to keep your meals exciting and satisfying. Stay active and engage in regular exercise to support your heart health. And remember to listen to your body, giving it the rest and rejuvenation it needs.

It's also crucial to regularly monitor your progress and consult with healthcare professionals to ensure you're on the right track. They can provide guidance, support, and personalized advice to help you navigate your unique health journey.

As you move forward, cherish the knowledge and empowerment you've gained from this meal plan. You now have the tools to take control of your coronary health and live a vibrant, heart-healthy life. Let this be the foundation for a lifetime of wellness and well-being.

Thank you for embarking on this journey with us. Your commitment and dedication to improving your heart health is commendable. Remember, you hold the power to reverse coronary artery disease and create a future filled with vitality and vitality. Embrace this newfound knowledge, continue to nourish your body, and let your heart thrive.

Wishing you a lifetime of heart-healthy choices and a future brimming with wellness and happiness!

With warmest regards,
Dr. Kaden Winton

Book description

Book Description:

Are you ready to take control of your heart health and reverse coronary artery disease? Look no further than "The

Coronary Artery Disease Reverse Cookbook: A 21-Day Meal Plan for Heart Health." This comprehensive and transformative cookbook is designed specifically for individuals seeking a practical and effective approach to healing their hearts through the power of nutrition.

What sets this cookbook apart is its evidence-based 21-day meal plan, meticulously crafted to support cardiovascular health and reverse coronary artery disease. Unlike other cookbooks that offer generic recipes, this book provides a well-structured and easy-to-follow plan, ensuring that every meal is packed with the essential nutrients your heart needs to thrive.

Inside these pages, you'll discover a collection of delicious, heart-healthy recipes carefully selected for their impact on heart health. From nourishing breakfasts to satisfying lunches and wholesome dinners, each recipe is expertly designed to reduce inflammation, promote optimal blood flow, and support your overall well-being.

But what truly sets this cookbook apart is the inclusion of a bonus meal planner. This invaluable tool allows you to organize your meals for the entire 21-day program effortlessly, eliminating the guesswork and saving you precious time. You'll have everything you need to succeed on your journey to a healthier heart with a clear breakdown of each day's meals, including breakfast, lunch, and dinner, detailed ingredient lists, and easy-to-follow preparation instructions.

Whether you're new to heart-healthy cooking or seeking a fresh approach to managing coronary artery disease, "The Coronary Artery Disease Reverse Cookbook" is your ultimate guide. Empower yourself with the knowledge and practical tools to change your diet and lifestyle.

Take the first step towards a healthier heart today. Embrace the power of nutrition, unlock the secrets of heart-healthy cooking, and reclaim your cardiovascular well-being with "The Coronary Artery Disease Reverse Cookbook: A 21-Day Meal Plan for Heart Health." Your heart will thank you.

Bonus

Food Journal

As an additional bonus feature in the *"The Coronary Artery Disease Reverse Cookbook,"* we present you with a valuable tool: a food journal. Keeping a food journal is an effective way to track your meals, monitor your eating habits, and gain insights into how different foods impact your well-being.

This beautifully designed food journal provides a dedicated space to record daily meals, snacks, and beverages. By jotting down what you eat and drink throughout the day, you can better understand your dietary choices and their effects on your body.

FOOD JOURNAL

Breakfast	Servings	Calories
	Subtotal	

Snack		
	Subtotal	

Lunch		
	Subtotal	

Snack		
	Subtotal	

Dinner		
	Subtotal	

Snack		
	Subtotal	

Total Calories From Food

FITNESS ACTIVITY JOURNAL

	Duration	Calories

Total Calories From Fitness

NOTES

FOOD JOURNAL

Breakfast	Servings	Calories
	Subtotal	

Snack		
	Subtotal	

Lunch		
	Subtotal	

Snack		
	Subtotal	

Dinner		
	Subtotal	

Snack		
	Subtotal	

Total Calories From Food [   ]

FITNESS ACTIVITY JOURNAL

	Duration	Calories

Total Calories From Fitness [   ]

NOTES

FOOD JOURNAL

Breakfast	Servings	Calories
	Subtotal	

Snack		
	Subtotal	

Lunch		
	Subtotal	

Snack		
	Subtotal	

Dinner		
	Subtotal	

Snack		
	Subtotal	

Total Calories From Food [   ]

FITNESS ACTIVITY JOURNAL

	Duration	Calories

Total Calories From Fitness [   ]

NOTES

FOOD JOURNAL

Breakfast	Servings	Calories
	Subtotal	
Snack		
	Subtotal	
Lunch		
	Subtotal	
Snack		
	Subtotal	
Dinner		
	Subtotal	
Snack		
	Subtotal	
Total Calories From Food		

FITNESS ACTIVITY JOURNAL

	Duration	Calories
Total Calories From Fitness		

NOTES

FOOD JOURNAL

Breakfast	Servings	Calories
	Subtotal	

Snack		
	Subtotal	

Lunch		
	Subtotal	

Snack		
	Subtotal	

Dinner		
	Subtotal	

Snack		
	Subtotal	

Total Calories From Food

FITNESS ACTIVITY JOURNAL

	Duration	Calories

Total Calories From Fitness

NOTES

FOOD JOURNAL

Breakfast	Servings	Calories
	Subtotal	

Snack		
	Subtotal	

Lunch		
	Subtotal	

Snack		
	Subtotal	

Dinner		
	Subtotal	

Snack		
	Subtotal	

Total Calories From Food

FITNESS ACTIVITY JOURNAL

	Duration	Calories

Total Calories From Fitness

NOTES

FOOD JOURNAL

Breakfast	Servings	Calories
	Subtotal	

Snack		
	Subtotal	

Lunch		
	Subtotal	

Snack		
	Subtotal	

Dinner		
	Subtotal	

Snack		
	Subtotal	

Total Calories From Food

FITNESS ACTIVITY JOURNAL

	Duration	Calories

Total Calories From Fitness

NOTES

FOOD JOURNAL

Breakfast	Servings	Calories
	Subtotal	
Snack		
	Subtotal	
Lunch		
	Subtotal	
Snack		
	Subtotal	
Dinner		
	Subtotal	
Snack		
	Subtotal	
	Total Calories From Food	

FITNESS ACTIVITY JOURNAL

	Duration	Calories
	Total Calories From Fitness	

NOTES

_____

_____

_____

_____

_____

FOOD JOURNAL

Breakfast	Servings	Calories
	Subtotal	

Snack		
	Subtotal	

Lunch		
	Subtotal	

Snack		
	Subtotal	

Dinner		
	Subtotal	

Snack		
	Subtotal	

Total Calories From Food

FITNESS ACTIVITY JOURNAL

	Duration	Calories

Total Calories From Fitness

NOTES

FOOD JOURNAL

Breakfast	Servings	Calories
	Subtotal	

Snack		
	Subtotal	

Lunch		
	Subtotal	

Snack		
	Subtotal	

Dinner		
	Subtotal	

Snack		
	Subtotal	

Total Calories From Food [   ]

FITNESS ACTIVITY JOURNAL

	Duration	Calories

Total Calories From Fitness [   ]

NOTES

Picture Links

https://images.pexels.com/photos/11112752/pexels-photo-11112752.jpeg?auto=compress&cs=tinysrgb&w=600&lazy=load
ls.com/photo/assorted-sliced-fruits-in-white-ceramic-bowl-1092730/

https://images.pexels.com/photos/10067237/pexels-photo-10067237.jpeg?auto=compress&cs=tinysrgb&w=600&lazy=load

https://images.pexels.com/photos/1833337/pexels-photo-1833337.jpeg?auto=compress&cs=tinysrgb&w=600&lazy=load

https://images.pexels.com/photos/3184188/pexels-photo-3184188.jpeg?auto=compress&cs=tinysrgb&w=600

Made in the USA
Las Vegas, NV
15 January 2024

84422320R00069